Management Poems by Madhoo

Vol. IV

Organizational Agility

The agility is important as against organizational inertia as below.

Running saga poem

A company Biggismallie has 12000 employees,

Big we may call, but others have 120000!

Small we may call, but some have 1200,

Running into losses,

As lethargy in employees,

Consultants pronounce inertia,

Change is constant, change now,

Soon comes an announcement,

Biggismallie wants to merge with Runnallie,

For its 1000 product lines,

For its 500 market segments,

For its 500000 customers,

Runnallie also announces to its employees,

Employees resist, signs of inertia

What is our gain?

For Biggismallie's technologies,

For its infrastructure,

For its office bases in 120 locations,

Biggismallie in the West,

Runnallie in the East,

Different parts of the world,

Both in a cross-border deal,

Runnallie is growing with growth inertia,

Biggismallie is declining with structural inertia,

Both have organizational inertia,

Runnallie's is good,

For growth need not change,

Biggismallie's is bad,

For employees need to change,

Good change, bad change,

Change is not inertia,

Merger creates momentum,

Momentum in products,

Momentum in processes,

New ones take charge,

Products, employees, rules, policies,

And merger finds its momentum,

With companies rewarding employees,

Games, contests, seminars, debates,

To make merger a success, creating ideas,

Competitors also throwing new innovation,

Challenging employees to tickle their brains,

Regulators pacing up with new rules,

Biggismallie racing up with cool,

Runnallie relaxing with previous growth,

Company then changes the name,

That changes the game,

New Runnbiggismallie enters the market,

With new investors, and new tickers,

With new buyers and new products,

With new standards and new capital,

Growth inertia uses experience success,

Structural inertia is replaced with vigour,

New change management process for the hour,

Boards merge, new directors come in,

Mission, vision, charters revisits begin,

Communication flows up and down levels,

Managers assist teams, and teams render members,

All learn about the new goals with fervour,

Employees start to understand the meaning,

Of the company as it stands for,

Customer satisfaction, social responsibility in the fore,

Employee satisfaction as onus on leaders,

To make sure all grow and flourish,

Career paths change, some downsizing,

Some hiring, some firing, some relocating,

Some resigning, some promoting, some stagnating,

Still the changes go on,

Failing ones go on training roll,

Quitting ones get some reprieve,

They say that theories need to be seen,

Resources, capabilities and locations matter,

Their satisfaction leads to buyer,

Their frustration beats to buyer,

Companies then start to shiver,

Without knowing that inertia is to hinder.

Now Runnbiggismallie is bigger,

Will this make it slower?

Runnbiggismallie is older,

Will this tire it sooner?

Companies live beyond a century,

Then only do they hurry,

Agility sees no age or size,

Organizations that don't work tire,

Employees retire, firms don't,

Customers leave, quality won't,

Brands change, customers change,

Markets change, environments change,

Uncertainty prevails, change prevails,

Explore and exploit to travails,

Else inertia prevails,

Runnbiggismallie has more locations,

Inertia can prevent new improvements,

Is not the vice versa?

New improvements can prevent inertia,

Whether the former is longer,

Or more or stronger,

Employees need to cooperate,

Competitors need also to,

Cooperate and collaborate,

Compete and strategize,

To keep pace globalize,

If not localize,

Combine to glocalize,

For inertia slows down decisioning,

It slows down transitioning,

It alleviates tasks exciting,

It mobs down true rivalry,

Competition becomes aggressive,

Rivalry becomes collusive,

Monopoly becomes exploitive,

Customers leave such in tandem,

For inertia munches knowledge,

To make it out-dated,

Technologies only operate,

Without any profits in making,

Some perish as rusted tools,

For inertia knows no life,

It decays corporate life,

Business becomes passive,

Firms become abusive,

Innovation is lost,

Products are copied at cost,

Prices don't appeal,

Buyers don't reveal,

For inertia can't understand,

No sentiments or detriments,

Learning is lost,

In the days of monotony,

Business repels,

At the sight of agony,

But employees don't respond,

For teams don't understand,

For bosses don't reprimand,

For organizational inertia won't stand,

The company sleeps, workers sleep,

Goals sleep, changes sleep,

Revenues sleep, sales sleep,

Returns sleep, investments sleep,

Leverage is lost, brand is lost,

Reputation is lost, money is lost,

Segmentation is lost,

Efficiency is lost,

Productivity is lost,

Strategy is lost,

Customer satisfaction is lost,

The company director stops,

But the consultant talks,

Runnbiggismallie is safe,

But these are alerts,

Continue to change,

To avoid rest in inertia,

Rest to strategize,

Motivate to revolutionize,

Work to innovate,

Govern to assimilate,

Corporate governance rules,

If new knowledge develops,

If new agility develops,

If new goals motivate,

Foreign firms invest,

Foreign direct investments rise,

If industries compete,

With sectors and inter-firm,

If returns promise gains,

If dynamic capabilities gaze,

If resources are effective,

Alliances are value-adding,

If strategies are divisible,

If actions are delegable,

If results are measurable,

Runnbiggismallie will be successful,

When strategies work with inertia,

Adopting growth,

Thwarting inflexibility,

Broaching new frontiers,

Taking inertia to promote growth,

Making inertia to hold knowledge,

Letting experience inertia to grow,

Companies continue to grow,

Industries then grow,

Economies grow,

Old knowledge must not go,

But remain with new,

Past experience must guide,

Without doubt on success,

Runnbiggismallie managers rise,

To imbibe the essence of strategy,

To welcome the benefits of inertia,

To eliminate the obstacles by inertia,

Taking the good change,

As leaving the bad change,

Welcoming the good inertia,

Changing the bad inertia,

Employees rise in job,

Performance starts improving,

Competition starts hailing,

Players start collaborating,

Knowledge sharing starts,

Leadership starts measuring,

All results meet targets,

Growth makes it to top,

Top-down and bottom-up,

Hierarchies become agile,

Stocks become responsive,

Markets start booming,

Investors start gaining,

Bourses start moving,

Trading rises in volumes,

And in margins and revaluations,

Risks start mitigating,

Contingent planning rises,

Risk management alters,

Bad Inertia falters,

Still nobody knows,

Age may slow down a firm,

Size may slow down the firm,

Employees may resist change,

Management may be reluctant to change,

HR team may be lethargic,

Administration may be less responsive,

Business may be less energetic,

A merger may infect with inertia,

A tough regulation may induce inertia,

A crisis may trigger inertia,

A slowdown may build in inertia,

A stagnant industry may breed inertia,

Government negligence may create inertia,

Exchange fluctuations may encourage inertia,

Currency rates may influence inertia,

Dooming Stock Exchanges may create inertia,

Changing organizational structure may create inertia,

Internal out-dated policies may feed inertia,

Out-dated technologies may feed inertia,

Continuous failures may breed inertia,

Sick units store inertia,

Bad product quality initiates inertia,

Low employee motivation levels store inertia,

Low customer satisfaction levels may trigger inertia,

Inaccurate timing may set in inertia,

Inefficiency may breed inertia,

Ineffective response increases inertia,

Low productivity is a symptom of inertia,

High attrition is a symptom of inertia,

Low employment rate is a symptom of inertia,

More defects, errors, wastage and low quality are symptomatic of inertia,

Low profitability is an effect of inertia,

Symptoms and effects may be causes
of inertia at times too,

Growth inertia continues,

With changes to the best,

Of the company's interests,

Of the employees' growth,

Of the business success,

Of the effective communication,

Of the raising benchmarks,

Of the sailing appraisals,

Of the collaborating competitors,

Making the best winning strategies,

Taking the best winning people,

Raking the best winning methods,

Baking the best winning sales,

Caking the best winning tactics,

Shaking the worst losing strategies,

Amidst all competitors, winning, losing,

Gaming with best winning strategies,

Industries, sectors, firms on noose,

Inertia that can make the game lose,

Inertia that can break the ice loose,

Inertia that can aid the best practices,

Inertia that can unearth old successes,

Inertia that can slowdown assembly,

Inertia that can increase over time,

Runnbiggismallie checked often,

One time, the labour was sloth,

Runnbiggismallie wondered why,

All tasks increased in duration,

All workers worked over time,

The factory looked shabby,

The bottlenecks were shabby,

The gadgets were faulty,

The trend began six months ago,

Sales fell, only then Manager awoke,

Employees were losing motivation,

They all needed innovation,

It was inertia in motion,

Manager changed rules,

Workers now get leaves,

With advances to go on vacations,

More work, less time, no commotions,

Supervisor involvement rises,

Workers get support and prizes,

Inspections to know views and
problems,

Machines are repaired,

New technologies are bought,

Activity increases, inertia decreases,

Workers work ways to innovate,

All these put labor inertia to rest,

Productivity rises, Efficiency increases,

Teams appease, workers release,

Markets realize, players apprise,

Inertia creates unrest in rest,

If not supported by change,

The same trends prevail,

If not changes to avail,

The products lose sheen,

The quality hides defects,

The employees disconnect,

The market timing takes ill-effect,

The sales decline,

The profits fall, often losses into red,

Customers reflect,

Loyalty to deflect,

Note inertia before it gets into rote,

Innovate in one way or the other,

Innovate in big or small,

Runnbiggismallie leaves this poem as a note,

To all firms in jettison,

Facing troubles in unison,

March into future,

With clear mission,

And a clear vision,

To make the business a success couture.

Madhoo is a Doctor of Philosophy in Strategic Management. The poem is adapted from the thesis work.

The poetic style adopted here is that of saga poetry.

www.ingramcontent.com/pod-product-compliance
Lightning Source LLC
Chambersburg PA
CBHW071602170526
45166CB00004B/1762

* 9 7 8 1 4 9 2 9 5 1 0 7 0 *